WITHDRAWN

Cover Girls

Cindy Crawford

Bob Italia

Published by Abdo & Daughters, 6535 Cecilia Circle, Edina, Minnesota 55439.

Library bound edition distributed by Rockbottom Books, Pentagon Tower, P.O. Box 36036, Minneapolis, Minnesota 55435.

Printed in the United States.

ISBN: 1-56239-106-2

Library of Congress Card Catalog Number: 91-0

Cover Photo: Retna LTD
Inside Photos: Globe Photos, Inc.   4, 7, 9, 22, 29, 31
                Archive Photos   26
                Outline Press Syndicate, Inc.
                The Bettman Archive
                Wide World Photos, Inc.   16, 20, 24

Edited by Rosemary Wallner

LIBRARY OF CONGRESS CATALOGING-IN-PUBLICATION DATA

Italia, Robert, 1955-
   Cindy Crawford / written by Bob Italia.
      p. cm. — (Cover girls)
   Summary: Describes the career of Cindy Crawford and how she achieved success as a fashion model. Includes her goals and personal beauty tips.
      ISBN 1-56239-106-2
   1. Crawford, Cindy — Juvenile literature. 2. Models, Fashion — United States — Biography — Juvenile literature. (1. Crawford, Cindy, 1966-. 2. Models, Fashion.) I. Title. II. Series: Italia, Robert, 1955- Cover girls.
HD6073.M772U5533   1992   659.1'52—dc20(B)   92-13692

International Standard Book Number:	Library of Congress Catalog Card Number:
1-56239-106-2	92-13692

Contents

Cindy Crawford—the face of the '90s.

Cindy Crawford

The Face Of The '90s

Supermodel Cindy Crawford is the hottest model to hit the glamor scene since Christie Brinkley. She has appeared on more than 200 magazine covers, has signed a multi-million dollar contract to be a spokesperson/cover girl for Revlon cosmetics, and has appeared regularly on her fashion show, *House of Style,* on the MTV cable channel. Rock star Prince even wrote a song about her on *The Black Album* called "Cindy C." Fashion magazines all over the world have dubbed her "the face of the '90s"—that means Cindy Crawford will be at the top of the fashion world for many years to come.

A Straight-A Student

Cindy Crawford was born in 1966 in the farm town of DeKalb, Illinois. Her father was an electrician. Her mother was a homemaker who took care of Cindy and her two sisters. "We never had any extras," said Cindy of her home life.

When Cindy was a first year student in high school, her father separated from her mother. "We were angry," she said. Still, Cindy had a happy childhood. But not having her father around made her work hard in high school. She consistently got straight A's, and fantasized about becoming the first woman president. Whatever she would become, Cindy knew she didn't want to stay in DeKalb and become a homemaker.

"I was rebelling against what my mother was at the time," Cindy said. "I loved her, but I didn't respect her. She didn't fight being a mom."

Cindy had always been a pretty girl. But she never wore makeup and didn't read fashion magazines. "Even when I put on just a little," she recalled, "the results were just disastrous." Becoming a model never occurred to her until she was a sophomore.

An employee from a local clothing store asked Cindy to be in a fashion show that would include some of her classmates. Cindy agreed.

"Some people got jealous," she recalled, "but it was worth it. I was still buying on layaway. We got a discount on clothes."

Afterward, things happened quickly for Cindy Crawford. A local photographer spotted Cindy in the fashion show and asked her to pose as the "Co-Ed of the Week" for a college newspaper. The photographer introduced Cindy to a local makeup artist. The makeup artist then told Cindy of a hairstyling demonstration by Clairol being held in Chicago and sug-

*Becoming a model didn't occur to Cindy
until she was a sophomore in high school.*

gested she participate. She could spend a weekend in Chicago, all expenses paid. Cindy agreed to go. Once in Chicago, a Clairol representative gave Cindy the phone number of a local model agency.

Cindy's "Flaw"

Cindy visited the agency. They arranged test photographs. Though she did well, the agency felt Cindy had one major flaw. Cindy had a mole near the left side of her upper lip. It was an "imperfection" the model agency didn't like. Cindy was turned down, and she returned to DeKalb dejected.

One of Cindy's test photos ended up in the office of Marie Anderson Boyd. Boyd was just starting her model agency and took an interest in Cindy.

"She had her hair up like a palm tree," recalled Boyd, "a kooky dress, a parasol, and a pucker."

Boyd went to DeKalb and called on Cindy's parents. She tried to explain that Cindy wasn't an average-looking girl. But Cindy's parents had their doubts and didn't want their daughter to pursue a modeling career.

"They thought I was a cute kid," said Cindy, "not a model."

Besides, Cindy had a good-paying job in DeKalb—working in the cornfields shucking corn for $1,000 a summer.

Cindy used to hide her mole. Now she is famous for it.

"Sort of like my job now," she said jokingly. "Worms, snakes, slugs, and bugs in your hair."

But after some persistence by Cindy, the Crawfords agreed to let their daughter take a chance.

"They gave me $500," said Cindy of her parents, "all they could afford to lose. I paid them back with my first check."

Boyd had photographs made of Cindy. The photographer made sure Cindy's mole was hidden in the shadows. But when Cindy showed up for interviews, the mole was there for all to see. So, Cindy was turned down a lot.

Many people suggested that Cindy have her mole removed. Cindy wanted to keep it. Boyd wanted her to keep it, too.

"Someday, they'll know you by that [mole]," Boyd told Cindy.

Cindy was glad she didn't have the mole removed. "Anything that sets you apart and makes you special is terrific," Cindy said. "For me it's my mole. You don't have to have blonde hair and blue eyes to be a top model anymore. Besides, most women have a mole *somewhere*. I think they can relate to mine, because it shows I'm not flawless."

Cindy finally began getting jobs—but not because of her mole. "I had no hips then," recalled Cindy, "but I had boobs."

Cindy's first job was a bra ad for Marshall Field's department store. When her fellow high school students saw the ad, it created a stir. Many of her classmates teased her about it and laughed at her. But Cindy maintained a professional attitude.

"If you knew what I was getting paid," she told her critics, "you wouldn't be laughing."

When she was a senior in high school, Cindy was getting many modeling jobs. She had to rearrange her school day so she could drive to Chicago every afternoon to work.

"She worked her tail off," said Boyd. "She was a pro from the beginning."

Soon after Cindy began working for Boyd, the agency merged with Elite Models in New York. At a party celebrating the merger, Cindy met photographer Bob Frame. Cindy hadn't done much in the way of modeling, but Frame had a feeling Cindy would become a supermodel someday. He began using her a lot.

"She knew what it was all about," said Frame. "You're a product. You have to maintain it and sell it."

As Frame had predicted, demand for Cindy increased. But Cindy was smart and didn't grab at every and any offer that came her way.

Meanwhile, Elite entered her in their Look of the Year contest. Cindy made it all the way to the national finals in New York. But she didn't win—although she could have if she said the right words.

"They asked you if you'd leave high school [to model]," she said. "I wanted to graduate."

At a very young age, Cindy showed the wisdom of an intelligent businesswoman. And no wonder—she went on to graduate as valedictorian of her class.

Cindy Goes To Europe

After graduation, Elite sent Cindy to Europe to see if she could make it as a model. Those who could survive the experience usually went on to become successful models. Those who didn't survive usually failed. Cindy Crawford lasted just three weeks.

Her first assignment was in Rome. There, the photographer for the Italian *Vogue* magazine wanted to cut and dye Cindy's long, dark, beautiful hair. At first she said no. But then she caved in under the pressure.

"I was crying," she said. "I wouldn't look in a mirror for two weeks."

Her next assignment was in Paris. Cindy thought it would be an exciting time for her—but it was anything but glamorous.

"They put four girls who don't speak French in a tiny apartment and leave them alone," she said. "I worked, but I had this short hair. I didn't know who I was."

Cindy began to doubt her career choice. She called her mother to see if she could reclaim a college scholarship she had originally turned down. But then Cindy got a job for British *Vogue* in Bermuda. "It was perfect," she said. "I could come back."

But it wasn't that easy.

"They had me lying in the surf for two hours with a mud mask on and waves splashing over my head," she recalled. "I didn't know I could say no. Those same people now would be 'Anything you want.' "

After that experience, Cindy had had enough of modeling. She was supposed to return to New York for another modeling job. Instead, she took the next flight to Chicago.

"I waited three hours and paid, like, $500 one way," she said. "But I was going home and I didn't care."

Cindy's Big Break

Back in Chicago, Cindy enrolled in Northwestern University to study chemical engineering. But while in Chicago, she met famous fashion photographer Victor Skrebneski.

"Cindy and I were doing amazing photos," said Bob Frame, "but then Victor started using her and she disappeared. Victor has a group he works with and is very loyal to. He's a really incredible teacher. His photographs are meticulous in detail, so the people in them learn how to work with themselves. If a strong girl comes around, Victor adopts her. Unfortunately, the good ones always leave."

For the next two years, Cindy—now 5 feet 9 inches and weighing 128 pounds—worked with Skrebneski and seemed very content. She was making over $200,000 a year. A college degree was no longer necessary, so she dropped out of Northwestern.

"It's cheap to live in Chicago," Cindy said. "My rent was half what it is now. I had a car. I was only two hours from home. It was great. But slowly, you start wanting more."

In 1986, Cindy frequently worked in New York City. But her ties to Chicago and Skrebneski were strong and she kept coming back. Then she and Skrebneski had a falling out, and Cindy decided to move to New York and work there full-time.

Cindy recalled the dispute in every detail because it happened on her twentieth birthday.

"I was leaving for New York that night," she said, "and I didn't want to work that day." But after two clients begged her to model for them, she agreed to work. The first client gave Cindy roses and a birthday cake. When she brought them to her second client—Skrebneski—he asked her, "Why do you have all that?"

After flying to New York the next day, Cindy was told that she had a big-money offer for a photo shoot in Bali. She called Skrebneski to cancel a photo shoot with him—and he got upset.

"That was it," Cindy said. "I understand his feelings. He made me. He did. But you can't make something and keep it for yourself. That was the break."

Cindy And Richard

Cindy Crawford worked hard in New York. She barely had any time for dating. She had dated the quarterback from her high school, but they broke up after she became a model.

"Our lives had totally diverged," she said. "This might sound bad, and I don't mean it to, but it's like a little kid who is finally ready to give up that security blanket. I can go to sleep by myself in the dark now."

In 1988, Cindy was invited to a Los Angeles party for singer Elton John given by photographer Herb Ritts. There, Cindy met actor Richard Gere.

"My mom pushed them together," recalled Ritts. "They got to talking, and it grew. He's changed her. He's a mature, intelligent guy. Anybody older, you learn if you're open to it. It's a very easy relationship. They're very sweet and good to be around."

Cindy is very protective of her private life and wouldn't discuss her relationship with Gere, whom she called her "friend in L.A." They were together ever since they met. She even had a fortieth birthday party for Gere.

Finally, on December 12, 1991, Cindy married Richard. But they did not have a traditional wedding. They eloped to Las Vegas and exchanged vows—and aluminum foil rings—in the Little Church of the West. The chapel reminded Crawford of the International House of Pancakes. Richard's agent, Ed Limato, was best man. Herb Ritts was the photographer.

Cindy Crawford and her husband, actor Richard Gere, at the 63rd Annual Academy Awards in Los Angeles, California.

After the brief ceremony—during which Richard promised to serve Cindy breakfast in bed for six months—Cindy and Richard had dinner at a nearby Denny's Restaurant. Cindy never wanted to make a big deal about her relationship with Richard Gere.

"I don't want to get scooped up in someone else's fame," Cindy said, "because then it's not mine. When I started modeling, no one knew me. I have managed to be this thing that appeared out of nowhere. I wasn't in clubs and being seen. I don't go to dinner every night when I'm on a trip, and photographers don't like that—models are supposed to be entertainment. I do my job. That validates me. My relationships are personal."

A Scare In New York City

In June 1988, Cindy Crawford got the scare of her life. It was 1 A.M. She had just returned to New York from a five-week working trip when she discovered that something was wrong with her Greenwich Village apartment.

Her things were out of place.

Someone had taken her telephone book. Her refrigerator was stocked with fresh food. And her bed was unmade.

Suddenly, the telephone rang.

"Don't be mad," said the man's voice. Then he listed the contents of Cindy's dresser drawers.

The man had gotten into Cindy's apartment. Somehow, while she was gone, he had made friends with Cindy's neighbors. Then he had taken an extra set of keys and visited her apartment every night after calling to make sure no one was there.

"I'm coming over," he finally said.

Cindy was scared. "I'm leaving," she told the caller.

"I can always find you," he said.

Thinking quickly, Cindy decided to play along. She agreed to meet him the next day at a restaurant. After hanging up, she sneaked out of her apartment and went to a friend's home where she called the police.

The next day, the man was waiting for Cindy at the restaurant. So, too, were the New York police. The officers arrested the man. Soon after, they discovered the man had been convicted of armed robbery.

"I had a mini-nervous breakdown," she said, "and then I was fine. I knew it shouldn't be a major event in my life. I wanted to tidy it up and get it taken care of. I don't have a listed phone. You don't learn until you make mistakes.

"He went on to confess," Cindy added. "I don't know why." The man pleaded guilty to second degree burglary and was sentenced to five years in prison.

Not A Typical Model

In spite of the scare, life in New York has been good to Cindy Crawford.

"She hit immediately, like a house on fire," said a friend. "She was very naive, but she got street-smart quicker than anyone I've ever met."

At first, people compared Cindy to a famous model named Gia. "I was 'baby Gia,' " she said, "but more wholesome. Gia was wild, completely opposite me. She'd leave a booking to buy cigarettes and not come back for hours. She's not living anymore."

"She was not your typical model," said photographer Marco Glaviano of Cindy. "She wasn't flirty. That slowed her down a little bit at the beginning, but it was good. That way, you don't get burnt out. There are lots of beautiful girls. But you need to have the brains to manage it. A lot of these girls don't use them because they've been told models are supposed to be stupid. And it's not a very stimulating business. They spend the day wearing lipstick and changing clothes. Even if they start smart, they can become stupid. Cindy's not afraid of being smart. That's a change."

"She's incredibly aggressive," added another New York photographer. "She always wants to be challenged."

When she moved to New York City,
Cindy became an instant modeling success.

"All the photographers love Cindy," said Sarahane Hoare, *Vogue*'s senior fashion editor. "She's not tricky—no bad vibes, no headaches. She's so professional, so thoroughly reliable, so kind. And always on time."

"Aside from the fact that she's extremely beautiful," said her agent, Monique Pillard of Elite Models, "she's professional to a fault. It's a pleasure to deal with her in my business. Modeling has changed a bit. People are watching their budgets. They can't take a chance on someone not performing—on not getting the picture. With Cindy, there's no chance. She honors her commitments."

Sol Levine, president of Revlon, had this to say about Cindy Crawford: "She is the consummate professional in her field. She's on time, well-informed, cheerful, understanding and eager to smooth things out if a backstage situation gets a bit tense. This is a lady who was raised in a home where good manners were taught and she uses them every day. She would succeed at anything she elected to do."

Cindy views herself this way: "My reputation in the business is that I'm always prepared. I don't come to work with bags under my eyes. I don't have chipped dirty fingernails. I make sure my legs are shaved and my hair is clean and trimmed. This is my job. Some people work in a bank. I model."

To capitalize on her growing popularity, Cindy modeled for a 1990 swimsuit calendar. It instantly became a bestseller. She posed for *Playboy* and *Gentlemen's Quarterly* magazines, did the famous swimsuit edition for *Sports Illustrated,* appeared on

Cindy hosts a beauty pageant for Revlon cosmetics.

the cover of *Cosmopolitan, Elle,* and *Vogue,* and did some high-paying Japanese soda pop commercials. Halston perfume signed Cindy for a sexy ad campaign. JH Collectibles signed her to model and be their spokesperson. And recently, Cindy got the biggest job of her career—a three-year contract with Revlon cosmetics that will pay her $600,000 each year. And let's not forget about that Pepsi commercial. Cindy has also appeared on *Late Night With David Letterman.* In addition, she hosts MTV's feature segment *House of Style.*

"It was a great opportunity," said Cindy of *House of Style.* "The work allowed me to show people another side of my character.

When you're a model, you are a face and a look. Adding a voice and a personality made me more of a person instead of a Barbie doll."

On *House of Style,* Cindy shows the latest fashion designs, interviews up-and-coming rock stars, and shows celebrity makeovers.

"It's about style but it isn't a typically boring 'and-long-skirts-will-be-back-in-the-fall' kind of thing," she said. "It's funky, hip, and young—basically, it's a colorful collage, much the same way MTV is."

House of Style takes ten to twelve hours to shoot. On the night before taping, Cindy studies her lines at home for an hour. The show doesn't interfere with her modeling.

All the success has not come easily. Recently, Cindy Crawford developed an ulcer. "I internalize a lot," she said. "I always felt I had to take care of everything myself. I didn't have an operation, but I take Zantac."

Thinking Of The Future

These days, Cindy Crawford thinks of the future—after modeling. While working for Revlon, Cindy can be found in Los Angeles where she spends time with her husband. She also reads for movie roles and takes acting classes.

*Cindy arrives at the Eighth Annual
MTV Video Music Awards in Los Angeles, California.*

"I'm sort of at the pinnacle of the model Cindy Crawford," she said. "A career should get better as time goes on. So modeling is out. I'd like to show another side of myself."

Cindy won't just take any movie role. She was offered a role in the movie *Wild Orchid* but turned it down because she would have to do a sex scene. She also read for *Beverly Hills Cop II.*

"I had to pretend I was holding a guy by his collar, say, 'Hey, squirrel brains,' and then pull a gun out of my leather jumpsuit," Cindy recalled. "I couldn't stop laughing."

Cindy did appear in *The Secret of My Success* with Michael J. Fox, but it was a very small part. "I'm in it," she said, "but if you blink, you'll miss me. It's not my whole life to be an actress. And I don't know I deserve it if I won't give up my firstborn for it. The one thing I know I want is children."

Though she is considered one of the most beautiful women in the world, Cindy Crawford can be insecure about her looks. "Most models, including myself," she said, "don't look into the mirror every morning and say 'God, you're beautiful.' We're extremely self-critical. I judge my looks by the number of bookings I get. Fortunately, these days I'm always busy."

Besides modeling and acting, Cindy spends her time reading, puttering around her New York apartment, and watching good rented movies with Richard. Though her schedule is hectic and personal time is precious, Cindy has no regrets.

"Face it," she said, "modeling's a great job. It's a great way to see the world."

Cindy autographs her best-selling swimsuit calendar.

Cindy Talks About Beauty

For Cindy Crawford, beauty starts with her diet. She does not eat any dairy products, fried foods, or red meat. And she doesn't drink, smoke, or eat acidic foods. Instead, she eats breads, vegetables, fruit, and fish. When she travels, she never eats airline food.

"I've never been to a country yet where I couldn't find something to eat," she said. "But just in case, I always pack dried fruits, cereal, and herb tea."

Cindy Crawford also places importance on exercise. She does calisthenics every morning, concentrating on her pectoral muscles, triceps, and abdominal muscles. She also rides a stationary bicycle for half an hour.

"Toning is so important for women," she said, "because we tend to get fleshy. Aerobic dance and running gave me headaches, so I quit. Exercise should be a release, not a mental strain."

Cindy is proud of her voluptuous figure.

"I wouldn't want to be stick thin," she said. "At the time of my high school graduation, I weighed 100 pounds and all my friends were so jealous. But it was a nervous, stressful time for me. My thyroid gland was going crazy and I had no energy. I didn't feel very good and I didn't look very good."

For her skin, Cindy uses steam, and goes to a salon for facials.

"My complexion is slightly oily," she said, "but the surface is dry from cleansers, heavy makeup, and plane air conditioning. I stand over a pot of steaming hot water every morning. After workouts, I'll sit in the sauna and rub off the flaky skin with a facial scrub."

When she's traveling, Cindy places a hot, wet towel over her face while bathing. To keep dark circles from forming under her eyes, Cindy stays away from caffeine and gets plenty of sleep—eight hours each night.

"I love to sleep," she said. "A lot of models go to clubs after work and stay out until three in the morning, but I'm not one of them. Getting enough rest is very important to me." A typical day for Cindy starts at 7 A.M.

Cindy also avoids the sun. When she has to be on the beach for a photo shoot, she uses an SPF 15 sunscreen on her face and body. When she can, she'll also wear a hat and T-shirt on the beach for added protection.

"I used to love to get tan," she said. "I'd pour on the oil and bake all day. Now I'm much more cautious. And I don't even miss the sun. When you have a tan, you look great for three days and then your skin starts flaking off."

Cindy is also careful about makeup.

To keep her skin healthy,
Cindy uses steam and avoids the sun.

"I didn't know very much about makeup before I started modeling," said Cindy. "But since then, I've learned that pink tones are the most natural and, therefore, the easiest to apply."

Though she is much more experienced these days, Cindy still does not use much makeup.

"Speed is the essence of my makeup plan," she said. "Mascara, lip gloss, and a little pink blush—enough to give my cheeks that just-pinched rosiness—are it for day. At night, I simply build on the basics for a more dramatic appearance."

To build on the basics, Cindy uses pink eye shadow on the upper lids and browbones, then a light line of brown shadow on the lower lids. She deepens the blush and brushes on pink lipstick.

"I rub lipstick on the widest part of my lips, then blot," she said. "That way, I never leave my 'mouth' on the rim of a glass." At night, she conditions her lips with a nontinted balm.

Cindy also likes to apply pink to her nails.

"Red dragon-lady claws aren't for me," she said. "I keep my nails medium-short, with paler pink polish for work and a brighter rose color in the evening."

A foundation is an important part of her complexion. "When I use it, I make sure the shade matches my skin tone exactly," she said. "And to avoid that mask effect, I blend the base thoroughly, then dust with translucent powder."

Cindy doesn't use a lot of makeup.

And yes, she also darkens that famous mole just a bit with a brown eye pencil. "I used to try to conceal it," she said, "but not anymore!"

Cindy Crawford's Address

You can write to Cindy Crawford at the following address:

Cindy Crawford
Elite Model Management
111 E. 22nd St.
New York, NY 10010